BOARDSAILING

John Heath

photographs by Tim Hore

Fernhurst Books

First published 1981 by
Fernhurst Books, 13 Fernhurst Road, London SW6

ISBN 0 906754 02 X

Acknowledgements

The publishers wish to thank Tabur Marine (GB) Ltd, Slough, Berkshire, for their help in the creation of this book, and also for their permission to reproduce the photographs on pages 18, 28 and 38.

Thanks are also due to Nick Hoare and Duncan Stone who posed for the photographs, and to the Dinton Pasture Country Club, Winnersh, Reading, where many of the photographs were taken.

Cover design by Margaret Hallam.

Composition by Allset, London
Printed by Hollen Street Press, Slough

CONTENTS

1 The gear

One of the great things about boardsailing is the simplicity of the equipment; you can rig your board in a few minutes and you don't have to be Superman to cope with it on your own.

The board shown here is a typical modern sailboard: other makes are very similar and can be rigged more or less as described here—see the manufacturer's instructions for variations.

A sailboard consists of an unsinkable board powered by a rig consisting of a mast, sail and wishbone-shaped boom, joined to the board by a pivot.

The board itself has a nonslip surface, a slot for the daggerboard and sockets into one of which the mast pivot fits. The fin on the underside helps the board sail in a straight line. The daggerboard stops the board being blown sideways; pivoting daggerboards are now available, which can be angled back when sailing with the wind behind you. Be careful to raise or pivot back your daggerboard in shallow water or you will damage it.

The rig is joined to the board by a rubber pivot which is inserted in one of the sockets in the board and which allows the rig to be angled in any direction. The fit between the mast pivot and the board is as vital as the adjustment of a ski binding—it must be loose enough to release if your leg is trapped between the mast and the board, but tight enough so that the mast doesn't keep jumping out. If the mast pivot does release, the mast plug prevents the rig floating away.

The sail has a sleeve sewn on the front edge, through which you slide the mast. Large sails need stiffening along the back edge; this is done by pushing battens into batten pockets sewn in the sail.

The rig is held together by three ropes—the inhaul attaches the boom to the mast; the outhaul pulls the back corner of the sail to the end of the boom; and the downhaul fastens the mast to the mast pivot as well as pulling down the front edge of the sail.

The uphaul is a knotted rope used to pull the rig out of the water. Fix the free end to the mast pivot with a length of elastic to keep it always within reach.

The wishbone shape of the boom allows the sail to set in a curve. Cleats on either side hold the ends of the outhaul rope and let you adjust the tension while sailing.

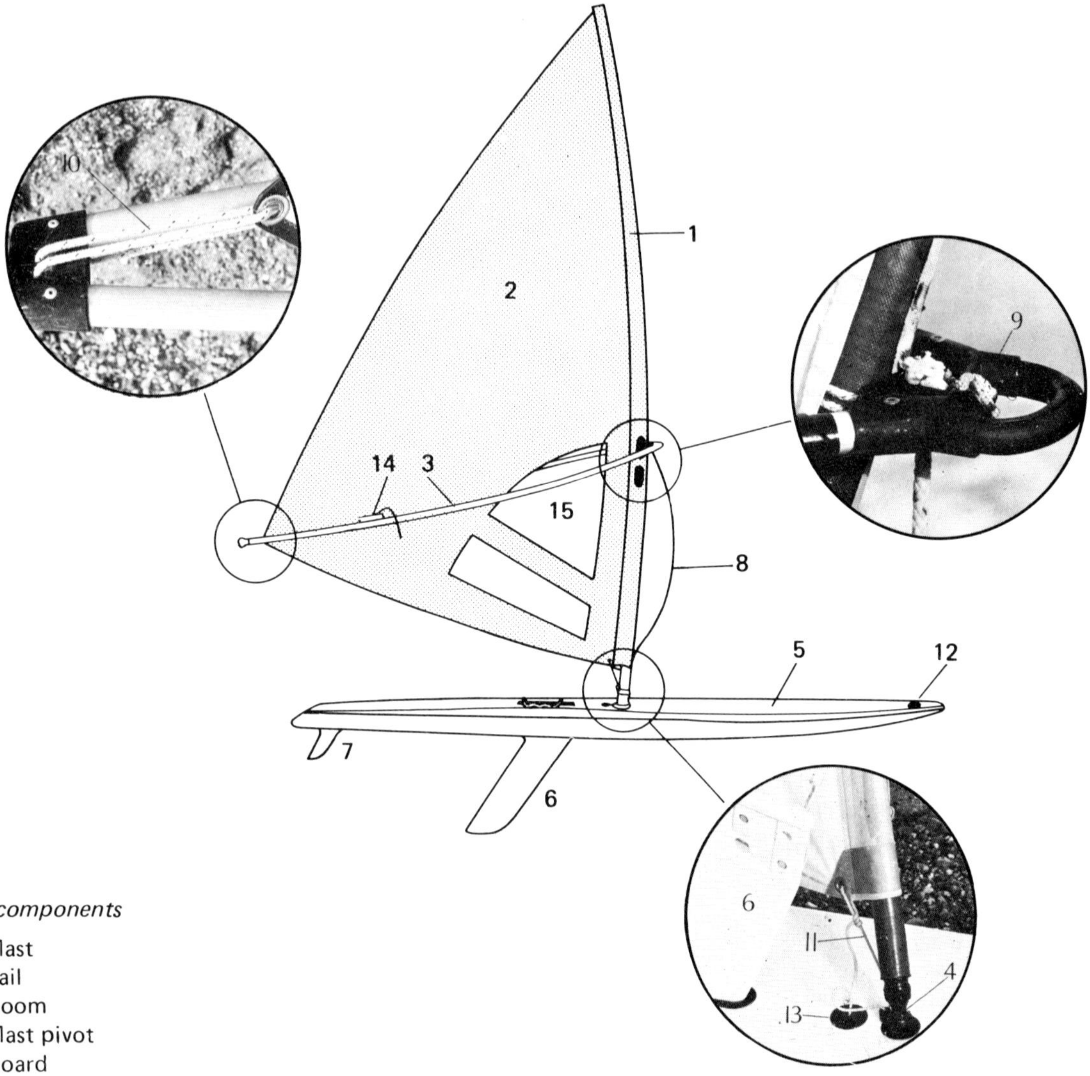

Main components

1 Mast
2 Sail
3 Boom
4 Mast pivot
5 Board
6 Daggerboard
7 Skeg (fin)

Ropes

8 Uphaul
9 Inhaul
10 Outhaul
11 Downhaul

Other

12 Towing eye
13 Mast retaining plug
14 Cleat for outhaul rope
15 Window

2 Getting it together

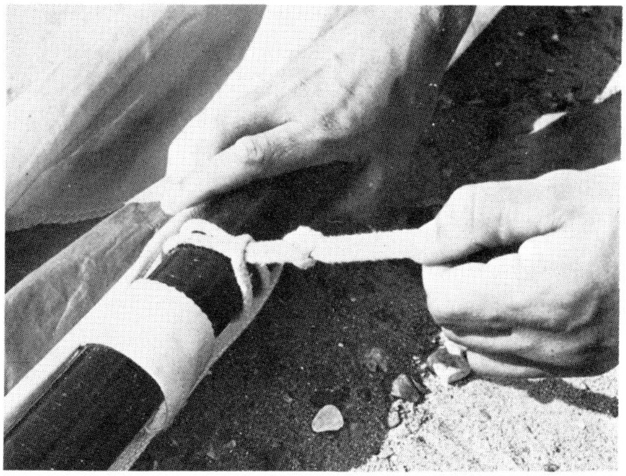

1 Push the mast through the sleeve in the sail. If you're using a large sail, put the battens into the batten pockets in the back edge of the sail.

2 Knot the inhaul around the mast through the slot in the sail. Adjust it to suit your height: if you're tall the inhaul should be near the top of the slot; put it near the bottom if you're short.

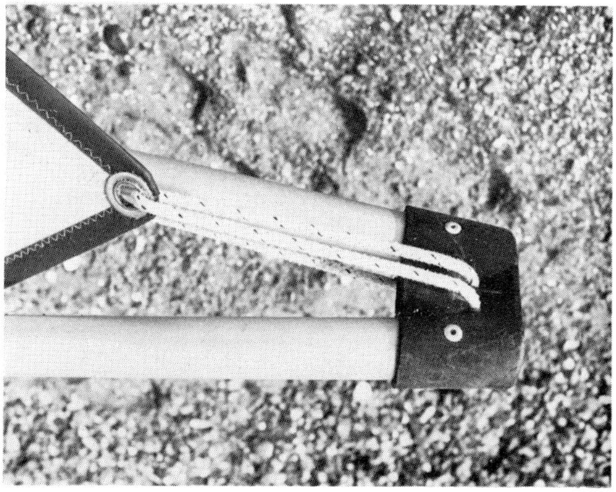

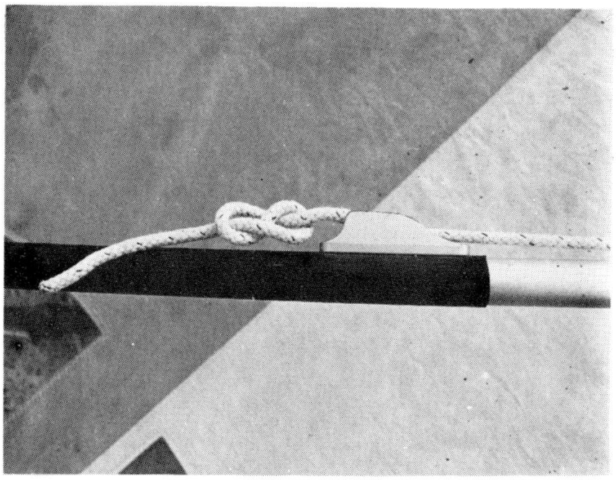

5 Rig the outhaul.

6 Push each end of the outhaul through its jamming cleat on the boom. Tie a figure-of-eight knot in the end of each.

3 Lay the boom along the mast and fix it to the inhaul, making sure the cleats are uppermost. Adjust the inhaul so that when the boom is raised into its working position, it is held fairly tightly against the mast.

4 Push the mast pivot into the mast. Tie the downhaul securely to the pivot—very tight for strong winds, less tight for light winds.

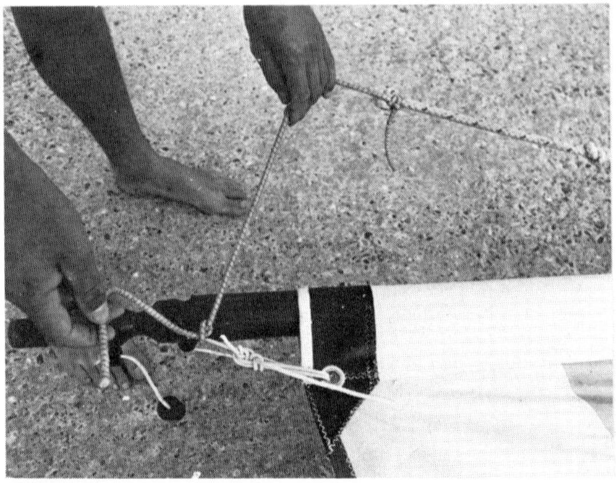

7 Knot the uphaul through its hole in the front of the boom. Tie the other end to the downhaul with a length of shockcord (elastic).

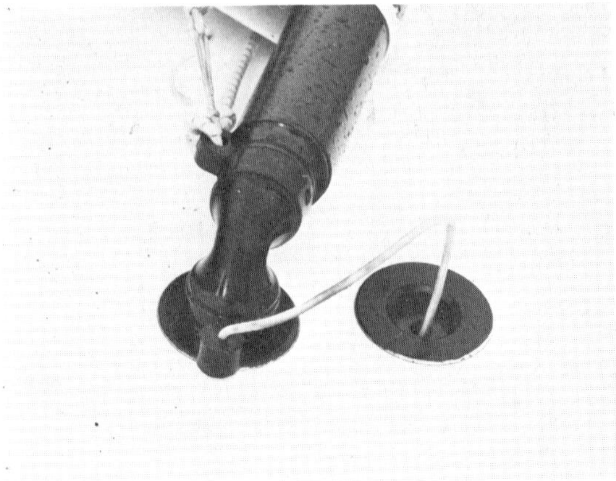

8 Push the mast pivot into the board—normally into the socket nearer the front of the board—and make sure the safety plug is firmly fitted into the other mast socket. Push the daggerboard into its slot, and you're ready to go boardsailing.

3 How it works

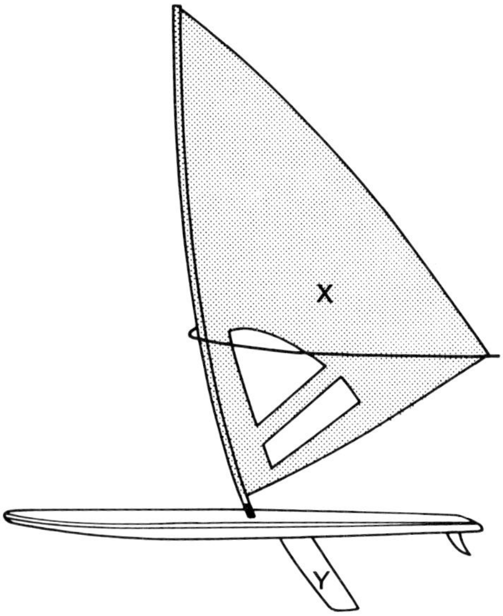

Take a close look at the photograph opposite.

- The boardsailor stands between the wind and the sail (the wind direction is shown by the streamer at the sail head—here from left to right).
- He leans back to balance the force of the wind on the sail. The force of the wind is driving the board forwards; the sideways force of the wind is resisted by the water pressure on the daggerboard.
- The boardsailor's front hand controls the angle of the mast to the board; his back hand controls the power in the sail.

How does the board sail?

The board moves forward as the result of three forces, of which you are one—and the most variable! These three forces are

the weight (or strength) of the wind
the weight of your body
the water pressure against your daggerboard.

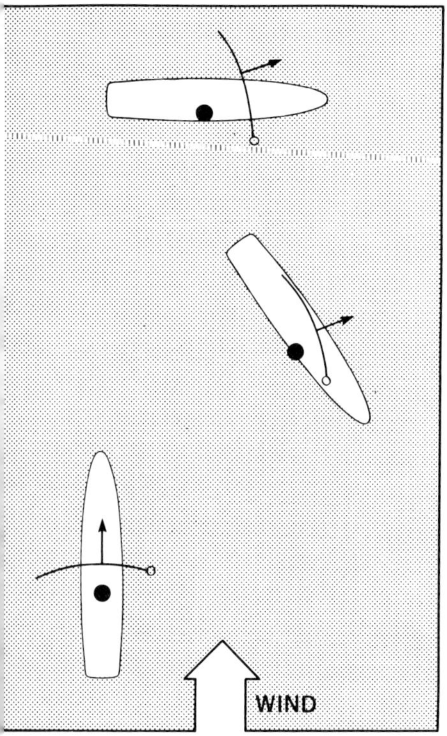

Wind

The driving force of the wind on the sail behaves as though it is concentrated at one spot, X in the top diagram. This force always acts at right angles to the sail, as shown in the lower diagram (you may like to make up the model at the back of the book to understand this more clearly). You will find later that you need to vary the angle of the sail to the board depending on which way you are sailing in relation to the wind.

Water

The water is not only there to support your board—it also presses on the daggerboard, preventing the board sliding sideways. This force also behaves as though it is concentrated at one point (Y in the first diagram).

Your weight

Something has to hold the sail up; all you have is the weight of your body. You will *not* be able to support the sail by

K485

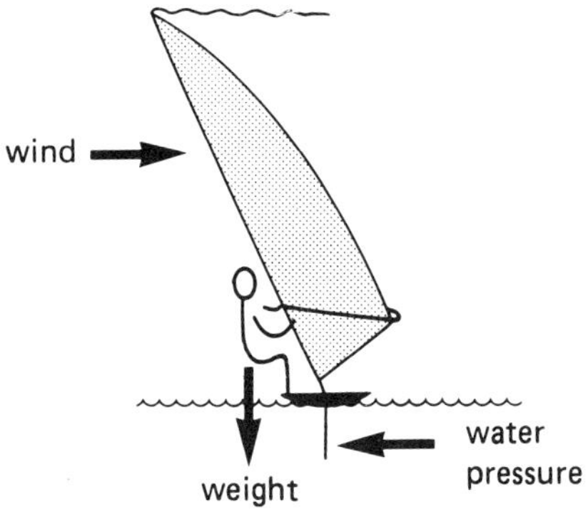

simply standing up and holding it—as most beginners try to do—you will just be pulled in forwards. Instead, lean the mast towards you (i.e. to windward) and lean back so your weight hangs from the boom. The stronger the wind, the more you will need to lie back to counteract it.

The drawing (left) shows all three forces in balance—this is your aim as a boardsailor.

How can I steer?

Not with the rudder—there isn't one! Instead, you can steer by changing the angle of the mast to the board. This is how it works.

The board always turns about its daggerboard. If the wind force X is above the daggerboard, there's no reason for the board to turn and it will sail in a straight line. If you rake the mast *forwards*, the wind force X comes in front of the daggerboard and the board will turn *away* from the wind. Raking the mast *back* turns the board *towards* the wind.

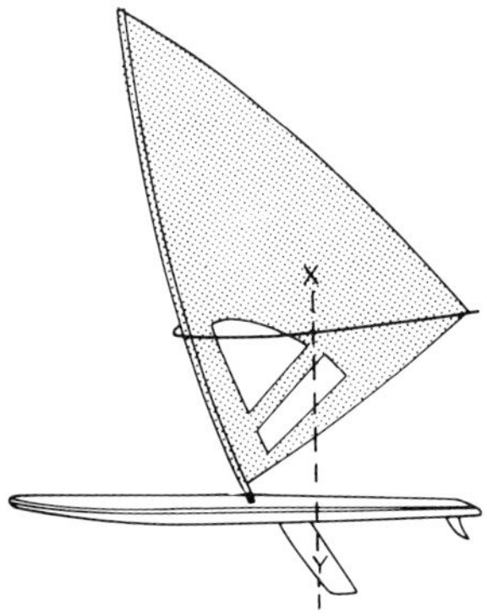

Perfect adjustment! The board is sailing in a straight line.

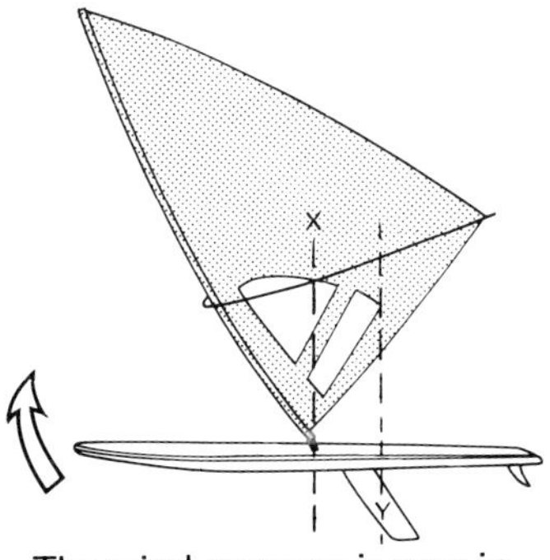

The wind pressure is now in *front* of the water pressure, so the board will turn *away* from the wind.

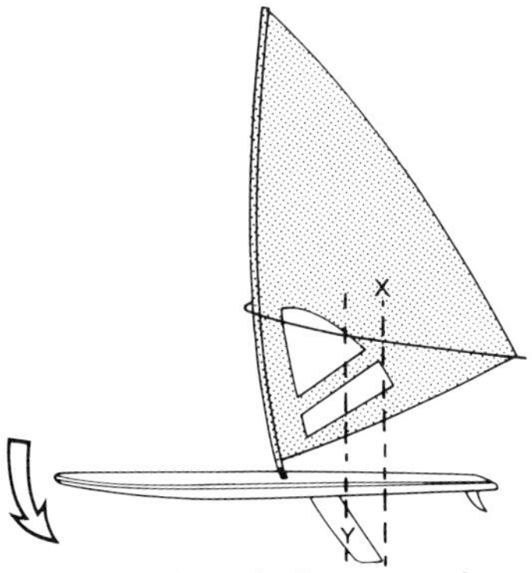

Because the wind pressure is now *behind* the water pressure, the board will turn *towards* the wind.

How can I stop?

Let go!

With both hands if you want to stop very quickly, in which case the sail will fall in the water acting as a very efficient brake.

Or let go only with your back hand so the sail blows directly away from the wind with no force on it, i.e. like a flag.

In a real emergency, simply fall backwards still holding the boom. You will stop in inches!

How can I tell which way the wind is blowing?

It's well worth attaching a streamer to the top of your sail so you can keep track of changes in the wind. If you get really muddled, let go with your back hand and let the sail blow away from you—that is the wind direction.

Can I sail in any direction?

You can sail across the wind, with it or towards it. The only direction you can't sail in is directly into the wind.

Reaching is sailing across the wind.
Beating is sailing towards the wind.
Running is sailing away from the wind.

Reaching

This board is reaching: the wind is blowing straight across the board, from behind the sailor's back. The mast is leant forward slightly to keep the wind force above the dagger-board—the board is sailing in a straight line. Notice that the boom is at about 45° to the centreline of the board.

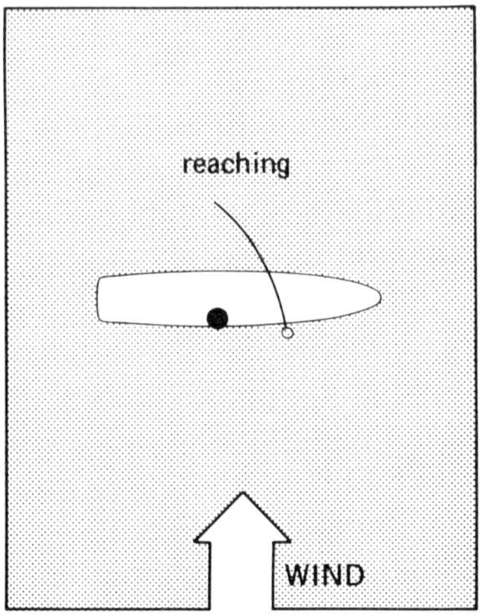

Beating

From a reach, raking the mast back turns the board towards the wind. The sail has to be pulled in as the board turns (to prevent the sail flapping), until the boom end is over the back corner of the board. This is *beating* and is as close to the wind as the board can efficiently sail. If the front of the sail starts to shiver, the board will have turned too close to the wind and the mast should be raked slightly forward until the board turns back and the sail stops shivering.

If the direction you want to sail in is directly into the wind, you will have to beat in a zigzag course. At the end of each 'zig' the board turns through about 90° –this turn is called a tack. Notice that the front of the board turns through the wind which then blows into the sail from the other side.

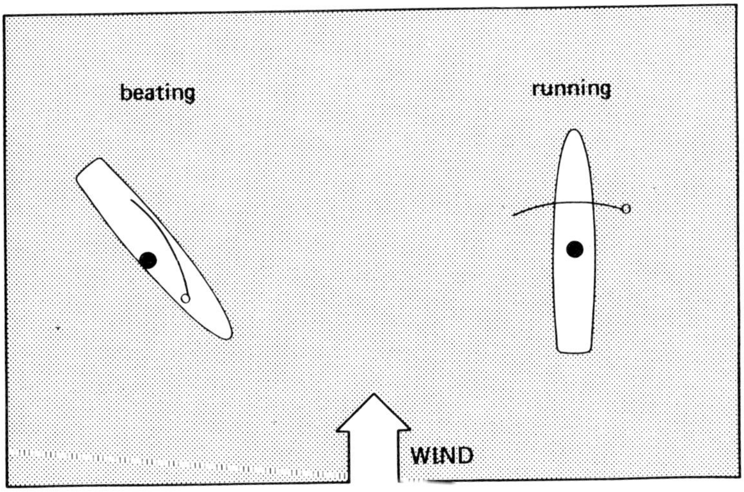

Running

Raking the mast forwards and gradually letting out the sail brings the board from a reach to a run. Here the wind is blowing from behind the board; the sail is held at right angles to the board, with the boom roughly horizontal, to keep the wind force above the daggerboard. Raking the mast to the left will turn the board to the right, and vice versa (the model may help to make this clearer).

If this boardsailor wants to turn still further to the left, he will need to gybe; here the back of the board turns through the wind, the sail is swung round forwards and pulled in on the new side.

All these points are summed up in the diagram opposite.

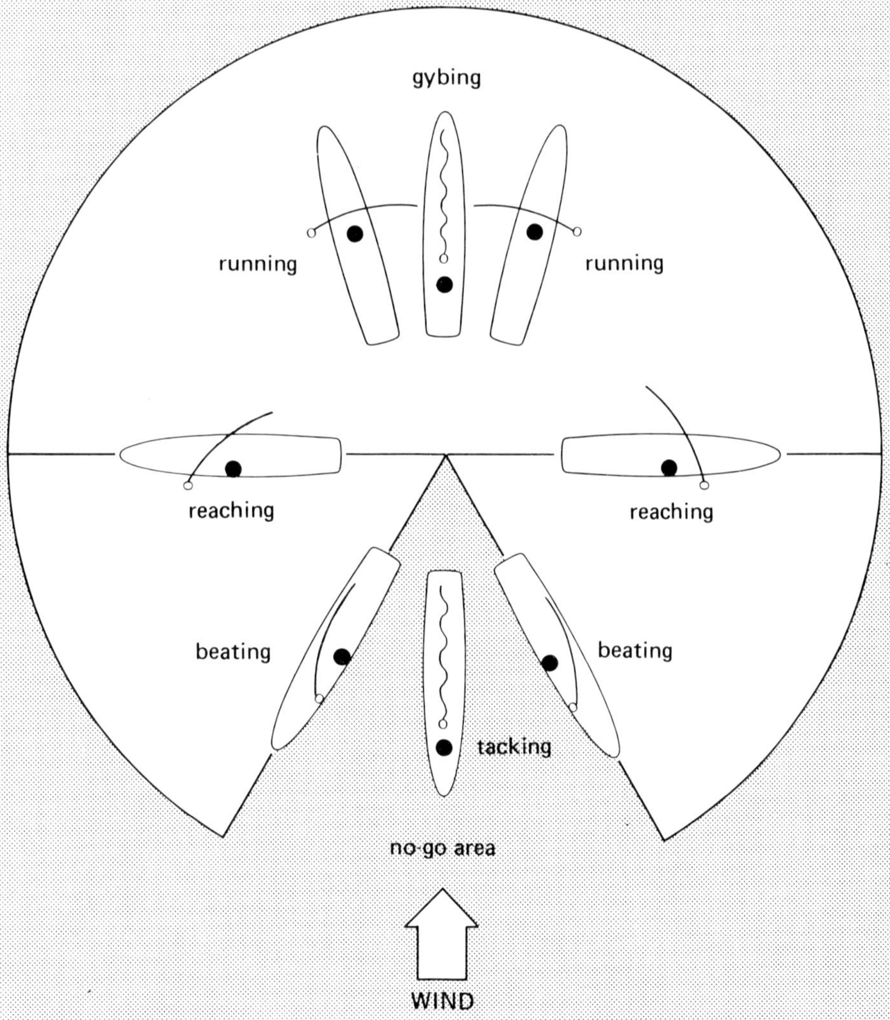
gybing
running
running
reaching
reaching
beating
beating
tacking
no-go area
WIND

Five-finger exercises

Before you take to the water, time spent practising handling the rig on shore—on the beach or even in your back garden—will pay immense dividends later. Whilst the sensation is not exactly the same as the real thing, the basics can be grasped at leisure and mistakes are not rewarded by an old-fashioned baptism!

If your first outing is via a boardsailing school—normally five hours of very worthwhile investment—then a dry-land simulator and a totally candid commentary will of course be provided.

Assuming a simulator is not available, place the mast pivot on the ground and stand on it with your foot. Pull the rig up using the uphaul and get into the start position as follows.

Photos 1-10: practising starting and tacking on dry land

PRACTISING STARTING

Stand with your back to the wind. Place your feet, shoulder width apart, in a line at right angles to the wind. Hold the uphaul in both hands, pull up the sail and let it blow directly away from you like a flag.

Decide which way you're going to 'sail'—let's say to the left. Make sure your right hand is at the top of the uphaul, with your left hand below it.

Reach across with your left hand to grab the boom about 15 cm (6 in) from the mast. This is now your 'front' hand. Don't hold the boom any nearer to the mast than this—you could trap your fingers.

Let your right hand drop from the uphaul.

Draw the sail to windward with your front hand until your hand is nearly against your left shoulder and the mast is angled across your left shin.

Stand like this for a moment, making sure that (a) you're in full control of the sail and (b) your feet and body are in the

1

2

3

4

5

correct position—feet across the wind, bottom tucked in, back slightly arched.

Brace your front leg; bend both legs, the back (right) one more than the front.

Now grab the boom with your right (back) hand, so that your hands are about shoulder width apart. Lean back and pull the boom towards you with your back hand.

If the sail pulls you *forwards* you need to lean the rig more to windward. Let out the boom a little by straightening your 'back' arm. You and the rig will start to fall backwards. When you are leaning back enough, pull in with your back hand again. You should now be lying back with the sail supporting you.

In a real gust, let go completely with your *back* hand. When practising this, don't move your feet from the centre-of-board position—you won't be able to step back onto the water! *Don't* let go with your front hand instead of your back —try it to see how disastrous this panic move can be.

If you find yourself falling over *backwards*, bend your knees and pull on the boom *sharply* with your back hand: this should pull your body back upright.

Stance

At all times keep your back straight, even arched rather than rounded. Besides giving the physiotherapist a day off, it gives you more control and a chance to adapt to gusts as they strike instead of being jerked forward into the water.

Only when hanging right out under the boom in strong winds should the arms be straight. In lighter winds keep them bent, allowing a degree of 'give' before reaching the end of your tether.

Sailing is an ambidextrous sport: for every kilometre you sail, you will have to sail a kilometre back in the opposite direction! So put in an equal amount of practice on either side of the sail. As you gain in skill, try 'tacking' when you change hands (see page 28). You can also try practising running (page 34) and gybing (page 38).

10

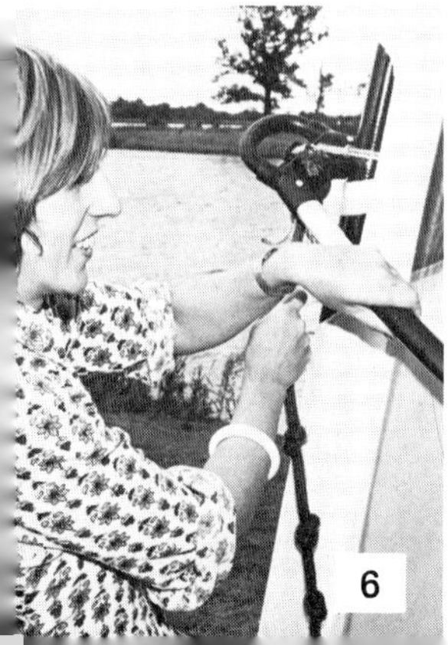
6

7

8

9

WALKING THE PLANK

It's well worth spending some time learning to stand on the floating board before you try raising the rig. If possible, *tether* your board by pushing a rope up through the back of the daggerboard slot and tying it to the top of the daggerboard; the other end can be tied to a mooring buoy or a stake on the bank. Otherwise, get a friend on the shore to hold the other end of the rope.

Leave the rig on the shore and get on the board by putting both hands on the centreline of the board and flopping onto it before getting into a kneeling position. Then get to know your board by standing up and practising balancing as the board wobbles; try to use your legs and particularly your ankles to balance with. Walk around and see how close to each end you can get and still stand up! Now jump around a bit. Practise standing sideways, rocking the board and compensating with your ankles. Learn the importance of keeping your weight on the centreline of the board—otherwise it will rock horribly.

Next, practise rotating the board: stand with your feet shoulder width apart on each side of the daggerboard and use your feet and legs to force the board round. Then rotate the board the other way.

1

2

5

RAISING THE RIG

Raising the rig is easiest if the board is at right angles to the wind. You can get into this position by pulling gently on the uphaul and rotating the board with your feet, until you have your back to the wind and the mast is pointing directly away from you.

Always keep your back straight and do all the work with your legs.

- Check your daggerboard is fully down. Place your feet one each side of the mast, about a shoulder width apart. Crouch down and grasp the uphaul.
- Gradually straighten your legs. Pause while the water drains from the sail. If the board seems determined to revolve, move slightly towards the end which is turning towards the wind.
- Once your body is straight, pull the uphaul in hand over hand. As the last corner of the sail leaves the water the weight of the rig will suddenly decrease, so be prepared for this or you'll fall in backwards.
- Continue to pull hand over hand until both hands are holding the uphaul just below the boom and quite close to your chest. You are now in the *start position*.

Photos 1-8: raising the rig

TURNING ROUND

Turning round is, for obvious reasons, a vital skill to have mastered before sailing off into a golden sunset, however inviting! It can be more difficult than straight line sailing, so now is the time to learn.

The board *can* be turned with your feet, as you have already practised; but it's much easier using the rig to help you. Leaning the mast either forwards or backwards makes the board turn about the daggerboard.

As an exercise, use this method to turn your tethered board through 360°.

- From the 'start position', lean the mast towards the back of the board. The weight of the rig will make it fall in that direction so that the sail fills very slightly. Because the wind pressure on the sail is now behind the water pressure on the daggerboard (see page 10) the front of the board will start to turn towards the wind.
- Keep leaning the rig and shuffle round the mast with small steps to help the board turn, always keeping to the windward side of the sail.
- Now change hands and rotate the board in the other direction.

Mastering this exercise will help you get lined up across the wind when you start sailing, as well as enabling you to turn round.

When you can turn the board easily, you are ready to unhitch and go boardsailing. But first have a short rest and think about the basic techniques you have just mastered and are about to use.

Turning the board through 360°

5 A first sail

Having learned to stand on the board and to rotate it, you can now combine these skills with your dry-land exercises. Try to control the sail as methodically as you did on shore, and try not to hurry: rushing the sequence of movements is a great way to test your buoyancy aid—again!

Before you untether your board, make sure that you have read the safety chapter on page 40, that you are properly dressed and equipped and that the conditions are suitable. If the wind is strong (over force 3) put in some more tethered practice and wait for a safer day. Your first sail should never take place without someone to keep an eye on you.

Launching

The board will blow away fast until it's fixed to the rig. The rig, on the other hand, will sit quietly and wait for you. So you must keep control of the board while launching. The easiest method is shown here—drop the rig in the water and go back for the board and daggerboard.

A more advanced technique suitable for launching in surf is shown on page 42.

Photos 1-3: launching

K 485

Photos 1-6: starting

Starting off

Check that your daggerboard is fully down, then raise the rig from the water until you're holding the uphaul just below the boom.

Rake the mast forwards or backwards until the board is at right angles to the wind. The sail will be blowing directly away from you, at right angles to the board. This is the 'start position'.

Check your feet—one each side of the mast.

Check your hands—the hand which will be the 'back' hand should be uppermost.

Now follow your dry land practice carefully: pass your 'front' hand over your 'back' hand and grasp the boom about 15 cm (6 in) from the mast (not closer).

Release the uphaul with your back hand. Draw the rig across your body until the front hand is almost against your front shoulder. You must be able to see the front of the board through the window in the sail.

PAUSE. Check the board is aligned across the wind, your stance is right and your balance perfect.

Brace your front leg—*bend both knees*.

Grasp the boom with your back hand, a shoulder's width behind your front hand; lean back slightly and pull in firmly with your back hand—and you're sailing!

If the board turns towards the wind, lean the rig forwards and push with your front leg.

If the board turns away from the wind, lean the rig back and push with your back leg.

Reaching

Since you started with the wind blowing across your board, and have kept sailing in a straight line, you are now *reaching*—i.e. sailing a path at right angles to the wind (as shown in the diagram). This is the easiest point of sailing, as well as the fastest and most fun!

Unfortunately, the wind can't be relied on to blow from exactly the same direction all the time (a streamer from the top of your sail will help you to keep track of windshifts) so you will have to adjust the sail constantly. Let the boom swing away from you until the front edge of the sail just begins to flap—then pull the boom in until the sail just stops flapping. (Try this with the model board: the idea is to get the 'wind force' pointing forwards as much as possible without letting the sail flap.)

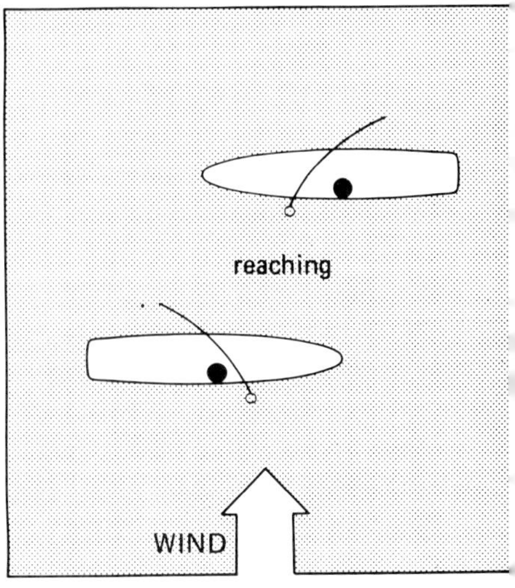

Thanks to your dry land practice, it should be easy for you to compensate for gusts by leaning further back, and to compensate for lulls in the wind by pulling hard with your back hand for a moment while bending your knees to bring your weight in over the board (left).

Check your posture: your bottom should be tucked in and any strain should be taken by your arms and legs. Your hands are about a shoulder's width apart—a little wider in stronger winds. Your feet should be in the 'start position' to begin with; as you improve, move them to the position shown below.

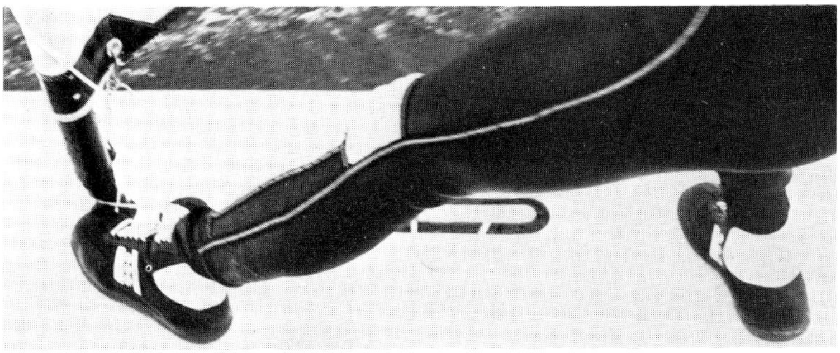

Steering

Steer the board by raking the mast towards the front or towards the back of the board as explained on page 10. The theory, however, was slightly simplified—you will find that in reality it is better to steer by raking the mast forwards and backwards *in line with the boom*.

To turn towards the wind, rake the rig back with both hands, push with your back foot and pull in with your back hand.

Turning away from the wind is less easy and the further you turn the more difficult it becomes. Rake the rig forwards with both hands and push with your front foot. Pull in with your sail hand to begin with, but as the board starts to turn, gradually let the boom swing out.

Practise steering a weaving course, turning the board first towards and then away from the wind.

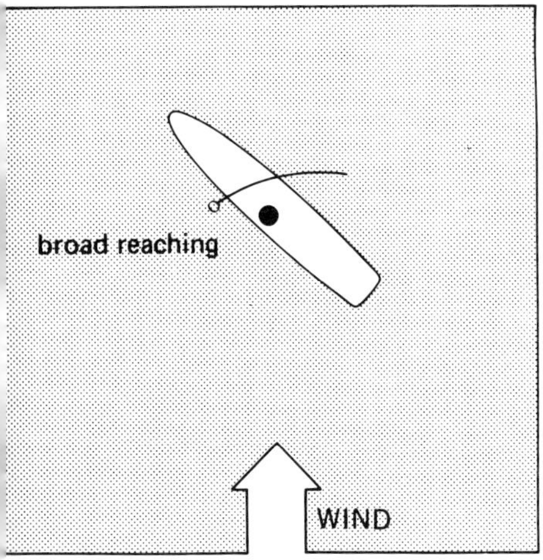

Broad reaching

When you have turned away from the wind, but not so far that the wind is directly behind the board (running), you are *broad reaching*. It helps to take out or pivot back the daggerboard for this point of sailing—but wait till you are a little more expert before attempting this!

SOME COMMON MISTAKES

Many beginners fail to lean the mast to windward sufficiently before starting off. Remember that you should be either upright or leaning back—if you lean forward like this you cannot support the sail and you may also damage your back.

A common problem is that the board turns straight into the wind as soon as you pull the sail in. Try holding the boom with your hands a little further away from the mast, so that the sail leans further towards the front of the board before you pull in with your back hand.

If this doesn't help, make sure that you are pulling in *really hard* with your back hand so that the wind force is acting at the centre of the sail.

If you find yourself falling in backwards, quickly pull in with your back hand and bend your knees to bring your weight over the board.

If things go wrong, let go with your back hand, *not* your front hand!

6 Turning round—tacking

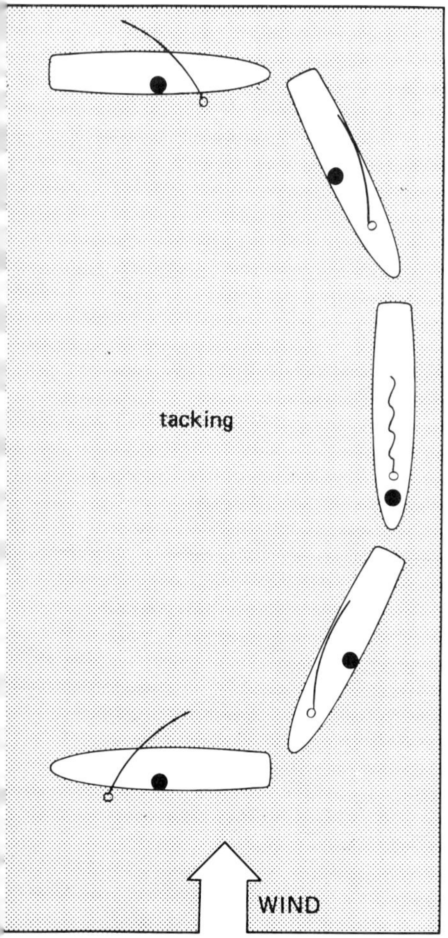

At last you can make the board sail in a straight line. You've even risked leaning back a little, and lived to tell the tale. Now you can try to turn round with a little more speed and style.

The easiest way to turn is towards the wind. When the front of the board has turned through the wind (that is, through the 'no-go area'–page 13) and you're sailing back the way you came, you have *tacked*.

Tacking–step by step

- Place your front foot just in front of the mast.
- Turn the board into the wind by leaning the mast right back and pulling the boom in with your back hand.
- When the sail starts to flap, let go with your back hand, pass it under your front hand and grab the uphaul.
- Shuffle both feet round in front of the mast. Grab the top of the uphaul with your front hand (both hands are now holding the uphaul). Tilt the mast to turn the front of the board through the no-go area.
- Keep turning the board by tilting the mast, shuffling both feet around the mast. Stop turning when you're in the 'new' start position, heading back the way you came.
- Now go through your start procedure. Reach over with your 'new' front hand and grab the boom, pulling it to windward across your body. Transfer your 'new' back hand to the boom, pull in and sail away.

Find it easy? Then you're ready to have a go at the quicker method of tacking described on the next page.

Photos 1-10: tacking

1

2

3

4

5

6

7

8

9

10

FASTER TACKING

You will need to tack fast in waves or if you race. The secret is to sail the board round, jumping around the mast at the critical moment.

- Turn–lean the mast back and pull the boom towards you. Aim to get the back corner of the sail in the water on your side of the board.
- Grab the mast with your front hand–keep pulling in the boom with your back hand to keep the board turning. The wind still blows into the sail from the 'old' side although the board has almost turned to its new course. Reach around the mast with your front foot.
- Transfer your back hand to the mast. Jump to bring your back foot around the mast.
- Pull the mast forwards with both hands. Reach across with your 'new' front hand and grab the boom, then transfer your 'new' back hand to the boom, pull in and sail away.

1
2
3

K485
K485
K485
6
5
4

7 Sailing towards the wind—beating

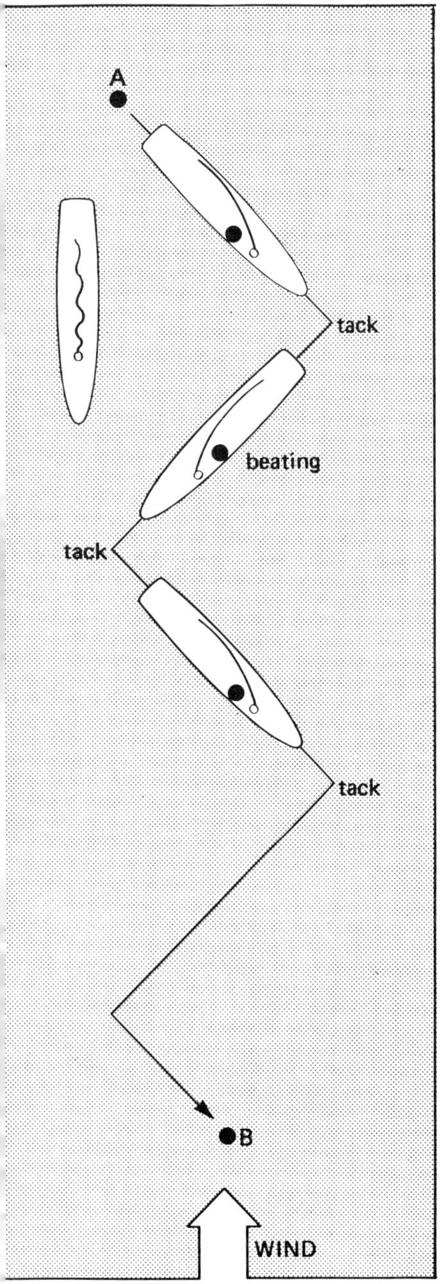

What is beating?

A board cannot sail straight into the wind (from A to B in the diagram). The sail will flap and the board will be blown backwards. The only way is to *beat*–to sail a zigzag course at an angle of about 45° to the wind. You are, literally, beating the wind which wants to push you back.

How close to the wind can I steer?

Always begin from the normal start position. Once the board is moving on a reach, you can lean the mast back to turn the board towards the wind, pulling in the boom as you turn, until the boom is almost along the centreline of the board–in light winds, even to the windward corner of the board. If you try to turn further, the sail will begin to flutter and the board will stop. Steer the board so that the front of the sail is just not shivering–you are now beating.

At the end of each leg of your zigzag course, you will need to tack–turning the front of the board through the no-go area.

Keep the daggerboard pushed right down when you are beating to stop the board being blown sideways.

To begin with, sail with your feet in the 'start' position; as you improve, move them to the position shown here.

8 Sailing away from the wind—running

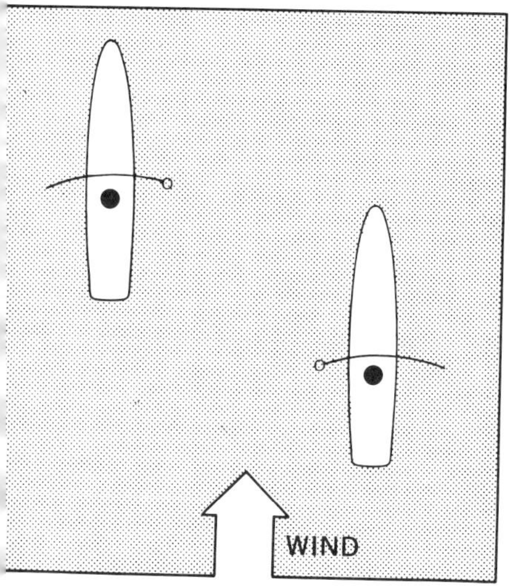

Both the boards in the diagram are running—i.e. they are sailing with the wind directly behind them.

Running is the most difficult point of sailing—the board becomes much less stable because the sail is 'edge on' to any rolling and does nothing to dampen it.

Getting on to a run

Begin from the start position as always. When the board is moving under control, rake the mast forwards and pull in with your back hand. As the board begins to turn lean back, let the boom *out* with your back hand and gradually rake the mast across the board with your front hand. Go on turning until the wind is blowing from the back of the board and the boom is at right angles across the board, and horizontal.

Hold the boom with your hands a little wider apart than usual so the boom cannot twist out of your grasp.

In light winds, keep your feet together as shown but in stronger winds adopt a 'fencing' stance—your front leg virtually straight, toes pointing forwards, while your back leg is bent and takes most of your weight, your back foot pointing across the board to keep it steady. Avoid the temptation to have a foot close to each edge of the board—a sudden lurch, all your weight on one foot, and the board capsizes!

Steering on a run

To sail in a straight line, the wind force must be in line with the daggerboard. To turn to the right, rake the rig across the board to the left, and vice versa. It also helps if you tilt the board slightly—push down with your left foot to turn right and vice versa.

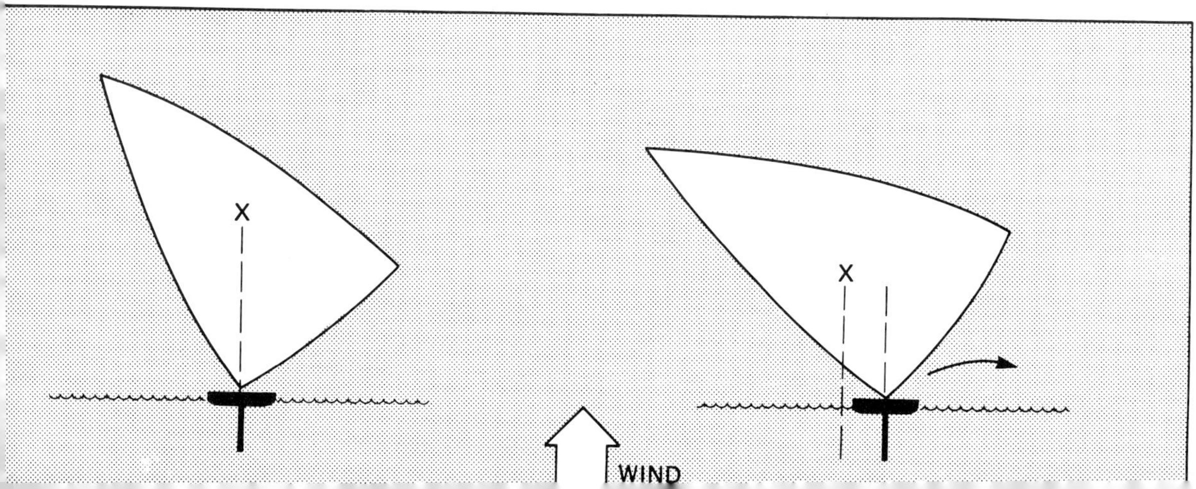

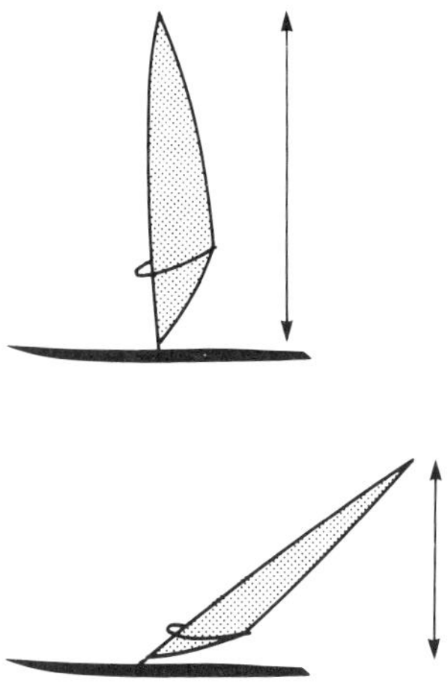

How can I stop being pulled over forwards?

If you find yourself being blown into the water on top of the sail, you must rake the mast *backwards*–this lets you lean well back so you can hang your body weight right under the sail. In a strong gust thrust with your front leg to lean the sail even further back; remember to let your weight forwards again when the wind passes!

In very strong winds, kneel down. In this position you can pull the rig well back over your head, and your centre of gravity is low. If things get really hairy you can sit or even lie on the board, to present the smallest possible sail area to the wind (see diagram).

I need to run to get home, but I can't do it. Help!

Don't panic. You can get home by holding onto the uphaul with both hands, letting the sail fly out forwards. Even when flapping, it will pull you home faster than your present efforts. If the wind is too strong even for this, simply drop the rig across the board (or better still, furl it), sit down and let the wind blow you ashore.

TAKING OUT THE DAGGERBOARD

Because the wind is behind you on a run, there is no sideways force to resist and the board will sail better without the daggerboard. If you have a pivoting daggerboard, simply pivot it back using your hand or your foot; if you have the lifting variety, pull it out, especially in strong winds–the board will then pivot about the fin, making it much easier to turn onto the run. However, taking the daggerboard out will make the board initially much less stable so beginners are advised to leave it alone until they are a bit more confident!

The sequence of photographs shows how it is done. As always, begin on a reach. Letting go with your back hand,

quickly bend down and grab the rope on the top of the daggerboard. Hook your back arm through the rope and grab the boom again, meanwhile raking the mast to keep the board across the wind.

As the sail fills, push with your front foot; then move back on the board, both feet pointing forwards.

9 Turning round—gybing

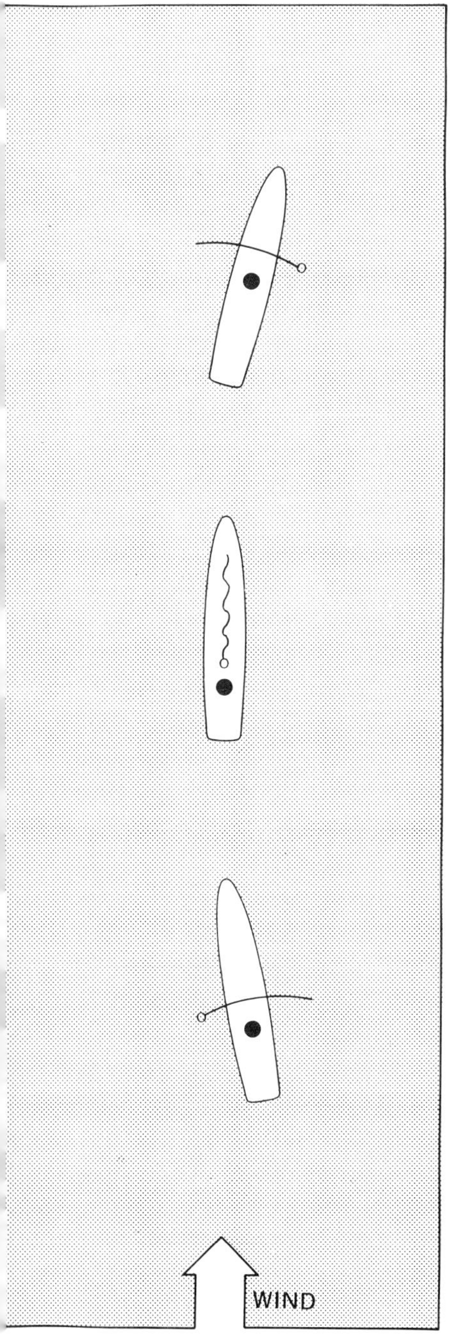

So far, you have been turning the board by tacking–i.e. the front of the board turns 'through' the wind. Gybing is another way of turning in which the *back* of the board turns through the wind: you will need this technique when sailing downwind. The sail is allowed to swing forward and then is pulled in so you are holding the boom on the other side.

How do I gybe?

- Turn the board until it's pointing directly away from the wind.
- Transfer your back hand to the uphaul (pass it under your front hand).
- Transfer your front hand to the uphaul.
- Lean the rig to turn the board to the new 'start' position (keep the rig out of the water by drawing the uphaul towards you).
- Follow the normal 'start' procedure; when you have picked up speed, you can turn back onto the run.

Photos 1-6: gybing

10 Safety

Preparation

Clothing. Dress properly for the worst conditions which might arise: a gentle breeze under a blue sky can quickly become a strong wind under grey clouds. In these circumstances you will need to be equipped with something more substantial than a swimsuit and optimism, if exposure isn't to become a greater risk than drowning. A wetsuit is virtually always essential, and ALWAYS WEAR A BUOYANCY AID.

Bare feet are only for the style-conscious expert who is not afraid to risk cold, bruised or even broken extremities; wear flexible sailing shoes or wetsuit boots with well-gripping soles and some outlet to drain water (most important) at sole level—don't be afraid to take a knife to the side of each boot.

If it is cold, add warm socks, gloves and a hat to this list.

Conditions. Check the wind strength and direction. If it is blowing offshore (from shore to sea) the sensible decision may be not to sail; by the time you admit to being in trouble you may be a long way from the shore. Find out the local weather forecast.

Choose a sail appropriate to the wind strength: a small sail without battens is much easier to control than a large sail with a rounded battened edge.

Know what the tides are doing (from tide tables). Boats at anchor lie head-on to the tide. Alternatively, look at the water swirling past buoys or posts.

Sail in company until you are proficient. Always tell someone where you are going if you're sailing on the sea or an estuary—and tell them when you've got back!

Equipment. Check your board, particularly the safety line connecting the rig to the board. It is a good idea to carry a spare thin line at least 2 m (6 ft) long, and it can be helpful to carry a light paddle—attach it with a bow line between the towing eye and the foot of the mast. Carry one or two small red flares.

On the water

Avoid swimming areas. Keep away from anglers' boats and divers' boats (flying code flag 'A'—a blue and white swallow-tail).

Look for a landmark when setting out from shore; something distinctive at 100 metres can be merely part of a hazy line at a kilometre! Don't go too far out at first.

Know the rules of the road (page 46).

Watch for changes in the weather, and keep an eye on your (waterproof!) watch so you know when the tide is turning. If the wind blows up, consider reefing—untie the downhaul and use it to 'brail up' the sail to the boom (see photo 1). Use your spare line to tie the mast pivot to the boom.

If you start falling in all the time, you are almost certainly more tired than you realise: come ashore.

In trouble?

Always stay with the board—never leave it to try to swim ashore, for instance. If the board and rig become separated, grab the board (*not* the rig) or it may blow away faster than you can swim; once you have climbed back on the board you can paddle after the rig—then ask yourself why it wasn't properly attached to the board.

If the wind is onshore, simply blow ashore by standing holding the uphaul, letting the sail flap in front of you like a flag (2).

If the wind is blowing roughly parallel to the shore, point the board towards the shore and pull the sail nearly up, letting the back corner trail in the water; the sail will partly fill, making you scud over the water surprisingly fast.

If the wind is offshore, furl the sail by undoing the outhaul and rolling the sail around the mast. Tie it to the boom with the outhaul and uphaul. Lie on the board and paddle ashore (3,4)—you can also paddle with your daggerboard or mast.

Another boardsailor can rescue you: position your board to windward of your rescuer and hang on to the base of their mast (5).

If you need to summon help, wave as shown (6,7). If no one sees you, let off a red flare.

3

4

5

6

7

11 Master class—strong winds & big waves

1

2

3

4

It's inevitable that you will have problems when you first sail in stronger winds or big waves. However, once you've got over the humiliation of becoming a beginner again, you're on the way to discovering what boardsailing is all about.

Launching

Launching in waves can be quite a problem. The secret is to keep the rig out of the water, and to climb on and get sailing as quickly as possible.

Push the board into the water on its *edge*, with the dagger-board in place; hold the mast high up, keeping the sail out of the water. When the water is deep enough, climb on without dropping the sail and get moving before a wave pushes you back. This is demonstrated in the photographs 1-4.

Getting started

A common difficulty with starting in strong winds is that the board turns violently into the wind as soon as you start to pull the boom in. If this happens, check the following.

- You are using a suitable size of sail.
- You are starting on a reach (i.e. the board is at right angles to the wind).
- You are drawing the mast right across the board to windward before you pull in the boom.
- You are pulling in really hard with your back hand.
- You are pushing your weight out and back as you pull in the boom.
- You are pushing hard with your front leg.

In very strong winds you may need to use a storm dagger-board. You can also experiment with putting the mast pivot into a different socket.

Beating

As you turn slowly towards the wind from the reach, remember that the board is much easier to steer when it is moving fast so don't point too close to the wind–go for speed.

You will need to stand close to the windward edge of the

board, and farther back than you have been doing in lighter winds. Steer over the waves by pushing with your back foot as you meet the wave, then push with your front foot as the board crosses the crest to get back on course.

If you do point too close to the wind the board will stall and stop—get back to the start position and begin again on a reach.

Photos 5, 6: strong-wind start

Using a harness. A harness takes the strain off your arms by allowing you to hang your body weight from the boom. Several different types are available; make sure yours has a quick-release catch. The one shown here consists of a hook which fits over a length of rope tied to the boom. The rope should be tensioned so that when sailing your arms are slightly bent. Position the ends of the rope so that your hook is in the centre of the rope when the rig is in balance.

Use the harness when beating; with practice, you will also be able to use it when reaching. Once you are sailing, hook on by pulling the boom towards you until the rope loop swings under your hook, then lean back.

Reaching and broad reaching

On a broad reach you'll need to pivot the daggerboard back or take it out (see page 37).

Keep your knees well bent, your feet well apart and let your legs flex as you sail over the waves. Try to ride the waves by pushing with your front leg and pulling in with your sail hand as the crest passes under the board, so that you shoot along the face of the wave. Avoid going down into the trough as the front of the board will bury itself in the wave ahead–if this is about to happen, move back to lift the front of the board; with luck you may be able to climb the wave ahead and ride on its face.

Running

Take out the daggerboard or pivot it right back. In very strong winds, sink to one knee or even lie on the board. Stay well back on the board and watch your balance. Gybes should be carried out when travelling fast down a wave (this reduces the wind force in the sail).

Broad reaching

Ride the waves by giving the boom a sharp pull towards you as a wave picks up the board—but don't pull the boom in too far: the sail won't support you if it is edge-on to the following wind.

Tacking

Keep the sail and your weight back for as long as possible going into a tack, so that you abandon the support of the sail for the shortest possible time while you step round the mast. Push or pull the rig to compensate for any lurching of the board as you turn. Get the sail pulling as quickly as you can on the new side.

Landing

Pivot the daggerboard right back or take it out and hang it over your arm; choose a small wave and ride it up the beach. Grab the rig and the board (as for launching) and drag them clear of the surf.

12 Rules of the road

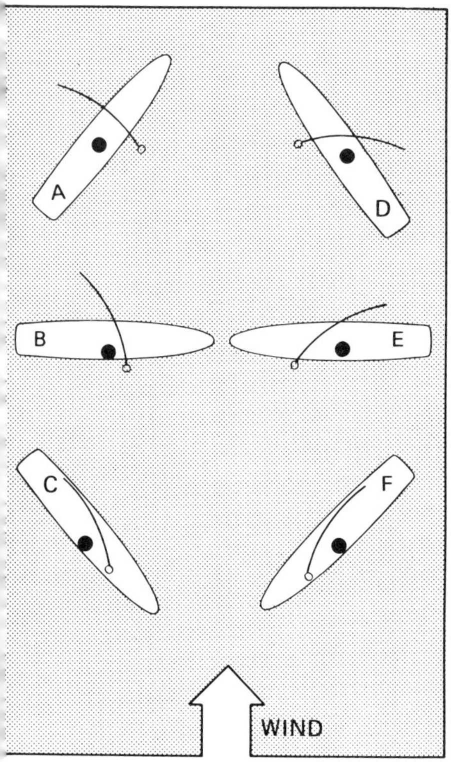

The rules of sailing are the same for sailboards as for any other sailing boat. A full discussion of them is outside the scope of this book, but there are three key rules you should know to keep you from doing too much damage to your fellow sailors.

Boards meeting on opposite tacks

A board is either on port tack or starboard tack. You are on port tack if your left hand is your 'front' hand; you are on starboard if your right hand is your 'front' hand. *A port tack board must keep clear of a starboard tack board.* Boards D, E and F are on port tack in the diagram and must keep clear of boards A, B and C which are on starboard.

Boards meeting on the same tack

If the boards are overlapped—i.e. if the bow of the following board is ahead of a line at right angles to the back of the leading board—then the *windward board must keep clear of the leeward board.* Board G must keep clear of H, I must keep clear of J and K must keep clear of L.

If the boards are *not* overlapped, then the *board clear astern must keep clear of the board clear ahead.* N is overtaking and must not sail into the back of M.

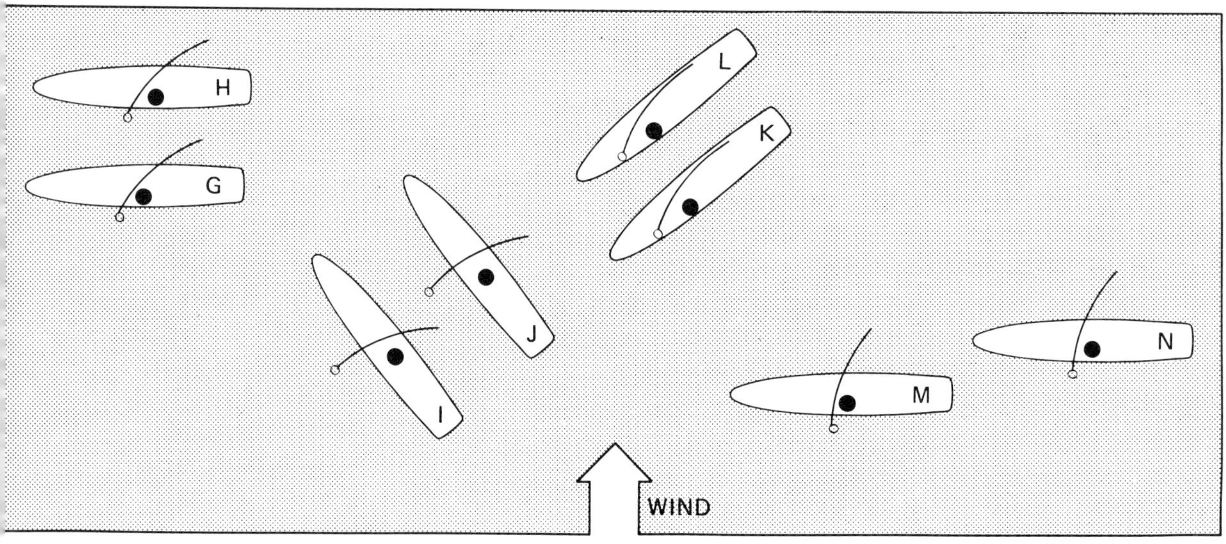